Williamson  Publishing

Where kids READ for the REAL world™

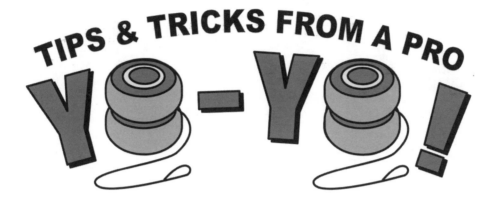

TIPS & TRICKS FROM A PRO
YO-YO!

Written & Illustrated by

RON BURGESS

Quick Starts for Kids!™

WILLIAMSON PUBLISHING • CHARLOTTE, VERMONT

Burgess, Ron.
   Yo-yo! : tips & tricks from a pro / Ron Burgess.
     p. cm. – (A Williamson quick starts for kids! book)
   Includes index.
   ISBN 1-885593-54-6 (pbk.)
   1. Yo-yos–Juvenile literature. [1. Yo-yos.] I. Title.

   GV1216 .B87 2001
   796.2–dc21

Quick Starts for Kids!™ series editor: **Susan Williamson**
Interior design: **Hilary Barberie, Monkey Barrel Design**
Interior illustrations: **Ron Burgess**
Cover design: **Marie Ferrante-Doyle**
Cover illustrations: **Michael Kline**
Back cover photography: **David A. Seaver**
Printing: **Capital City Press**

Williamson Publishing Co.
P.O. Box 185
Charlotte, VT 05445
(800) 234-8791

Manufactured in the United States of America

10 9 8 7 6 5 4 3 2

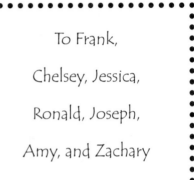

To Frank, Chelsey, Jessica, Ronald, Joseph, Amy, and Zachary

2001025835

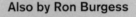

Also by Ron Burgess

Williamson's *Quick Starts for Kids!*™
BE A CLOWN!
*Techniques from
a Real Clown*

Contents

Let's Go Yo-Yo!_____ 4

Kids' Yo-Yoing Questions ...
    With Answers from a Pro!____ 5

What Makes a Yo-Yo Go?_____ 7
    The Spin on Yo-Yo Designs_____ 8
    The String Thing_____ 11
        How to Replace a Yo-Yo String_____ 12
        Taking Out Knots_____ 14

Quick Starts to Yo-Yoing____ 15
    Getting Started_____ 16
        Pat-a-Cake_____ 19
    Winding Ways_____ 20
        The Hand Wind_____ 20
        The Thumb Start_____ 21
        The Choo-Choo Wind-Up_____ 21
        The Two-Finger Start_____ 22
        The Kick Start_____ 22
        Walking the Plank_____ 23

Solo Yo-Yo _____ 24
    Gravity Pull_____ 25
    Sleeper_____ 26
    Walk the Dog_____ 27
    Creeper_____ 28
    Forward Pass_____ 29
    Around the World_____ 30
    Cowboy_____ 31
    Around the Corner_____ 32

Over the Falls_____ 34
Hop the Fence_____ 35
UFO aka Sleeping Beauty
    and Flying Saucer_____ 36

Dynamo Yo-Yo _____ 38
    Breakaway_____ 39
    Rock the Baby_____ 40
    Loop the Loop_____ 42
    Three-Leaf Clover_____ 43
    Shoot the Moon_____ 44
    Elevator_____ 45
    Monkey on a String_____ 47
    Flying Trapeze_____ 48

Ho-Ho Yo-Yo_____ 49
    Jumping the Dog Through a Hoop____ 50
    Dog Bite_____ 51
    Slurping Spaghetti_____ 52
    Runaway Dog_____ 53
    Dragster_____ 53
    Skyrocket_____ 53
    Buzz Saw aka Rattlesnake, Walk the
        Duck, and Shoe Shine_____ 54
    Walk the Cat_____ 56
    Skin the Cat aka Tidal Wave_____ 57
    Playing the Bass_____ 58
    Bow and Arrow_____ 58

Resources_____ 60
Index_____ 61

LeT'S GO YO-YO!

So, you were given a yo-yo and you never did know what to do with one of them. Lately, you've been trying to do all those smooth tricks, and you just can't get the hang of it. What gives?

Well, let me give you a hand! Not a real hand, of course — though sometimes when you're doing yo-yo tricks it feels like you do need three hands — but some useful tricks and techniques that will have your yo-yo spinning through space!

What's the secret? Step-by-step practice. Once you have the "hang" (or twirl) of one step, move on to the next. Even the easy tricks can seem difficult at first, until you break them down into individual steps. (I've been yo-yoing for years, and I still have trouble with *Walk the Dog* — the easiest trick in the world.)

You don't have to do the tricks in the order given here, although I'd begin with some of the solo yo-yo tricks on pages 24–37.

But we're getting ahead of ourselves. Before you do any tricks, read the information on string and taking out knots. It will make your yo-yoing life much simpler, and you'll learn things about yo-yos you might never have guessed!

For example, did you know that the yo-yo is a great toy that's been around just about forever? (Some people believe, as toys go, that only dolls have been around longer than yo-yos have.) And yo-yoing is an international sport that's being considered for entry into the Olympics!

Whether it's a toy, a sport, a hobby, or a gift you feel you should dig out of your drawer, yo-yos are loads of fun and can be enjoyed by anyone — young or old, girls, boys, men, and women.

So, let's go yo-yo!

Kids' Yo-Yoing Questions... With Answers from a Pro!

Q: I don't get it. I see other kids smoothly yo-yoing — even my uncle is great at it — and mine always stops. Clunk. Spin. Stop. What's the secret?

A: There are basically five secrets to yo-yoing, but they're each pretty easy to learn. The first trick is to understand that you need to control the string (page 11). The second trick is practice. The third, practice. The fourth — you guessed it! — *practice!* The fifth? Keeping in mind that yo-yoing isn't brain surgery, the fifth is the easiest — *having fun!*

Q: Does it make any difference if my yo-yo is inexpensive?

A: You've probably heard the saying "All that glitters is not gold," so a smart yo-yo spinner like you isn't likely to be fooled. Inexpensive yo-yos are just as much fun and a lot easier on the allowance!

Q: Some yo-yos are made out of wood and others out of plastic. Is one better than the other?

A: That all depends on your yo-yo preferences (and your bank account!). Yo-yo prices range from 89¢ (yes!) to more than $100 (ouch!). Ask your friends if you can try out theirs. Get a feel for how each one operates. A yo-yo that they might like, you may not, and vice versa. In the long run, it all depends on what you prefer.

Q: With all the different kinds of yo-yos out there, how many do I need?

A: As you practice and improve, you may want to spend more on a particular kind of yo-yo that has special features. But in the beginning, you need only one. And to choose, just ask yourself: Is this the kind of yo-yo that's going to make me *want* to play with it?

Quick Starts Tips!™ from a Pro

The Way to Go Yo-Yo

If you're considering what kind of yo-yo to start with, I suggest a simple, no-frills yo-yo. Beginners who go straight to the high-tech models usually don't learn the basics that enable them to develop control of their yo-yo. If you start out on a simple, fixed axle yo-yo, you'll be able to learn the control and techniques that will make you look like a yo-yo pro in very little time!

Kids' Yo-Yoing Questions... with Answers from a Pro!

Q: My granddad gave me a great wooden yo-yo that he played with when he was my age. I want to use it, but the string broke and now it's all frayed. Do I need to buy a new yo-yo?

A: Not a problem! Several yo-yo manufacturers sell new yo-yo string, so you can keep on using your favorite wooden yo-yo or the one your best friend gave you that lights up when it spins. (See *Resources*, page 60.)

(P.S. Old yo-yos are very popular collectible items, and some of them can fetch a pretty hefty price, so hang on to dear ol' Granddad's! And believe it or not, it will be much more valuable with the original string left on it, even though you'll want to change the string if you're actually going to use it.)

Q: How fast can my yo-yo go?

A: Well, how much do you want to practice? Professional yo-yo spinner Dale Oliver got his yo-yo to spin 14,400 times in one minute! That's one *fast* yo-yo! (Now how do you think they were even able to measure that many spins? Beats me!)

Q: What's the difference between a *sleeping* yo-yo and a *dead* yo-yo?

A: A *sleeping* yo-yo is one that is spinning at the end of the string, whereas a *dead* yo-yo is one that has stopped spinning at the end of the string.

Q: I've seen kids on the playground make their yo-yos "sleep" for several seconds. They try to break each other's records all the time. What's the longest anyone's been able to do that?

A: World Pro Yo-Yo Master Hans Van Dan Elzen — Yo Han, to his friends! — set a world record in 1998 of 7:08, with a very special yo-yo. Then, Rick Wyatt practically *doubled* that record with a sleeping time of 15:06 at the 2000 World Championships, using a specially designed yo-yo with an aluminum rim.

The rest of us can do a respectable 10 to 30 seconds with a regular wooden, fixed axle yo-yo (page 9), and maybe one minute with a ball bearing, rim-weighted, transaxle, aluminum yo-yo (page 9). But who knows? With enough practice, you might be the next world-record holder!

WHAT MAKES A YO-YO GO?

The yo-yo sure has come a long way since kids played with them in ancient China and Greece thousands of years ago. It's been all around the world (and even into outer space, on the space shuttle *Atlantis* in 1992!). Along the way, it's gone through some pretty interesting changes, but it's so cool to think that something so simple has remained popular for so long!

The Spin on Yo-Yo Designs

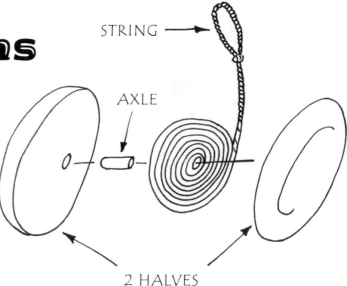

STRING

AXLE

2 HALVES

It seems that after a few thousand years, whether you're using a tournament yo-yo, a slimline yo-yo, or a butterfly yo-yo today, you're still pretty much playing with the same four parts that kids did in ancient China and Greece:

But wait — if you're thinking there might have been a few improvements over the years, you're right! There are several modern designs, and each one has its own advantages.

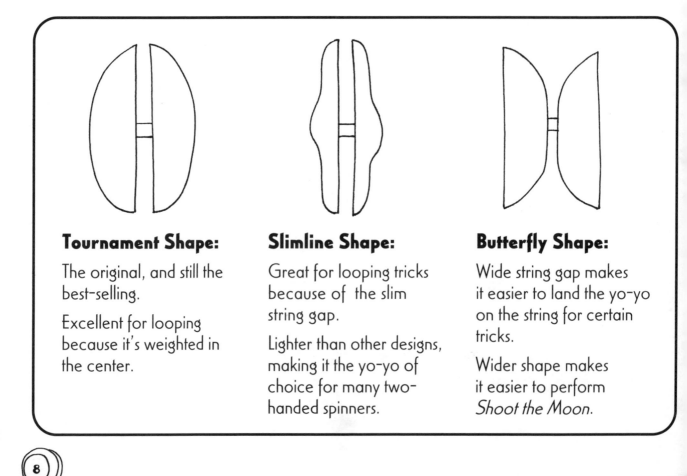

Tournament Shape:

The original, and still the best-selling.

Excellent for looping because it's weighted in the center.

Slimline Shape:

Great for looping tricks because of the slim string gap.

Lighter than other designs, making it the yo-yo of choice for many two-handed spinners.

Butterfly Shape:

Wide string gap makes it easier to land the yo-yo on the string for certain tricks.

Wider shape makes it easier to perform *Shoot the Moon*.

And that's not all. See that axle that connects the two halves? There are differences there, too, hidden between the two halves:

TYPE	DESCRIPTION	ADVANTAGES
Fixed axle yo-yos	halves are not meant to be removed	usually inexpensive, the best yo-yos to learn tricks on, and used by both beginners *and* professionals
Dismountable (take-apart) yo-yos	developed in the late 1980s so the halves could be taken off the axles	removable halves make it easier to replace strings
Transaxle yo-yos	have a special axle covering that rests on ball bearings	sleep easier and longer than other yo-yos
Centrifugal clutch yo-yos	introduced in the early 1980s, built-in clutches separate so yo-yo spins freely. When the yo-yo slows down, built-in springs push the clutches back together to grab the axle and return up the string	automatic return feature means that if thrown properly, these yo-yos sleep and then return on their own

Quick Starts Tips!™
from a Pro

Axle Anxiety

With so many different axles and yo-yos out there, how do you know which one is best for you? Well, that depends on which kinds of tricks you think you might enjoy. Wooden fixed axles are great for making your yo-yo "sleep" (spin) or for doing looping tricks. Even better, though, for sleeping tricks is the transaxle. (You may have to pick up a few extra babysitting jobs because it's also the most expensive.) The centrifugal clutch one automatically returns, which makes it fun for beginners, but not good for difficult tricks.

So it seems even yo-yos have gone high-tech! Who knew?

What goes down,
must come up!

YO-YO UPS AND DOWNS

Have you ever wondered exactly how a yo-yo works? When you throw a yo-yo, you create *momentum* (the energy that makes an object move). This momentum forces the yo-yo to travel down the string. Once it's at the bottom, your tugging creates *friction* (the force created when one solid object rubs against another). This makes the string grab the axle, enabling the yo-yo to return up the string.

Now you might think that gravity would keep the yo-yo at the bottom of the string. But the friction created by your tugging puts into play a scientific truth called Newton's Third Law of Motion: *For every action, there is an equal but opposite reaction.* In this case, it means that what goes down, must come up!

The String Thing

The string is the most important part of the yo-yo because it's the part that lets you yo-yo. Aside from your hand and wrist, the string works the hardest, so always make sure you use a clean yo-yo string. It should be changed when it looks dull, gray, brown, worn, or frayed (don't wait until it's black or worn-out — yuck!) because a dirty or frayed string will make it difficult for your yo-yo to do tricks the way you'd like it to.

* String becomes frayed and worn at the axle (inside the yo-yo where you can't see it) and near your yo-yo finger. Check the color and condition of your string to see if it's frayed or worn, because if it breaks at a frayed or worn place, the yo-yo could literally go flying. At 35 mph (56 kph), it could bonk your head pretty hard, break your glasses, or do serious damage to teeth or eyes — not only yours but others'! With this in mind, you're probably already realizing that it's not a good idea to yo-yo in front of a window, a mirror, your mom's favorite lamp, or anything else that could be broken.

* Change your string before it breaks. A good rule of thumb is to change it after about an hour of yo-yoing. With some people this could be in two or three days, and with others it could be in two or three hours. It depends on how much you play with your yo-yo.

* Here's the string thing that every yo-yo expert knows: Use only *real* cotton yo-yo string — not the string that you use to wrap packages with. Most toy stores or yo-yo vendors sell yo-yo string. You can also buy yo-yo string in bulk from yo-yo makers (see *Resources*, page 60).

Spaghetti String

Throwing the yo-yo always tightens the string if you're right-handed and loosens the string if you're left-handed. Eventually, you can end up with a real mess called "spaghetti string." It looks like tangled-up spaghetti (without the meatballs). The easiest way to untangle it is to remove the yo-yo from your finger, hold the yo-yo in your hand, and let the string hang down in front of you. As it starts to untangle, you can help it along by gently pinching and pulling the string down. Avoid forcing it, though, or you could end up with a big, ugly knot.

Sometimes, the spaghetti string just won't untangle. In that case, it will have to be replaced. It's not the end of the world, though — just consider it an opportunity to start fresh!

How to Replace a Yo-Yo String

First Things First

Of course, you have to remove the old string. You can do this by pinching the string about 1"–2" (2.5–5 cm) from the yo-yo. By twisting the yo-yo *counterclockwise*, you can separate the two strands that make up the string. This creates a loop large enough to slip the yo-yo out. If there are knots around the axle and you can't get the string off, you'll have to work on the knots. Use an opened paper clip or a long needle to work out the knots, but be careful not to scar the inside of the yo-yo or the axle — or stab your hand! Please don't use a knife or any sharp items.

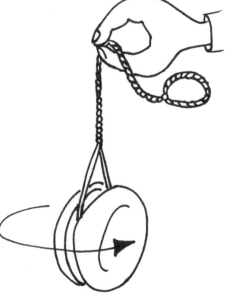

TWIST COUNTER-CLOCKWISE

YO-YO! Tips & Tricks from a Pro

Putting on the New String

With your yo-yoing hand, pinch the new string about 3" (7.5 cm) from the unknotted end. With the opposite hand, unwind the section below your pinch to separate the two strands that make up the string. Place a couple of fingers into the opening to create a loop large enough to slip in the yo-yo. Slide the yo-yo into the loop, but don't let go of the pinched end with your yo-yoing hand. Let the string wind back to its natural twist while it tightens around the axle. Make sure that the string winds evenly so that there are no kinks or bulges. If there are, you'll notice them immediately, so you can just unwind and start again. You probably won't need to, though; it's easier to do than it is to explain!

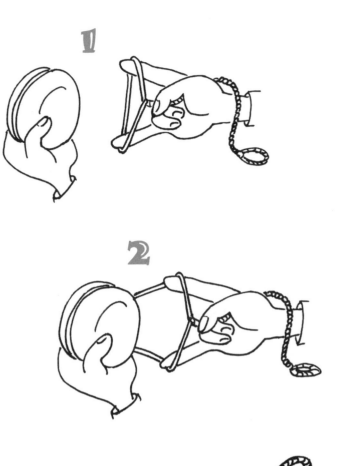

The string might be a little loose when you first use it (see page 14 for tightening tips). You might have to throw the yo-yo a few times and twist it clockwise to get it to work properly (or counterclockwise if you've twisted it too tight to enable it to sleep). Some strings take more time to break in than others do.

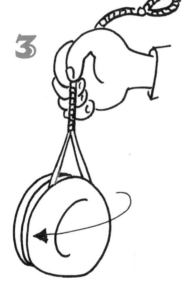

Check in your yo-yo's instruction book. Some yo-yos have to be double- or triple-looped over the axle, but as a beginner, you don't need to know about that yet. (When you're ready, though, you'll find instructions included in the manuals that come with these special yo-yos.)

What Makes a Yo-Yo Go?

Taking Out Knots

One of the things that yo-yo experts know is that you should never use your yo-yo with a knotted string because using it makes the knot tighter and more difficult to undo. It also affects your yo-yo's performance. So taking out knots is the first trick you can learn!

If the string is knotted along its length, try to remove the knots with your fingernails. If that doesn't work, use an opened paper clip, a pushpin, or a sewing needle to work on the knot. Be careful: Don't stab yourself in the finger, and be sure *never* to use a knife or any other sharp instrument. (You'll hurt yourself and your yo-yo!)

Most yo-yos today are dismountable (take-apart) yo-yos, so you can simply separate the halves to fix knots around the axle. To fix knots on yo-yos that don't come apart (fixed axle yo-yos), you'll have to use an opened paper clip or needle while taking care not to scar or scratch the axle.

If the string can't be unknotted, well, just think! Now you have a chance to practice replacing your yo-yo string!

Quick Starts Tips!™ from a Pro

Wide-Awake Yo-Yo!

The tension of your string will have a lot to do with your yo-yo's performance. Sometimes, it just gets wound so tight that it can't sleep. (Sound familiar?) But if it's too loose, the yo-yo won't return to you.

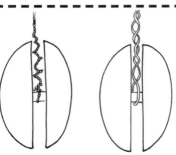

No biggie! This is any easy thing to correct. To loosen the string, let the yo-yo hang down in front of you until it stops spinning. Twist it about 10 times *counterclockwise*. If it still doesn't "sleep," twist it a couple more times and try again.

To tighten the string, let the yo-yo hang down in front of you until it's "dead" (not spinning). Twist it *clockwise* about 10 times. If it still won't return, twist it a few more times and try again. Just be careful not to tighten it too much or the string will snap.

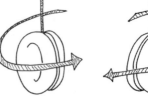

LOOSEN
COUNTERCLOCKWISE

TIGHTEN
CLOCKWISE

QUICK STARTS to YO-YOING

So, now we're back to the beginning: You've got a yo-yo. Your uncle has always been great at it — and you don't know how to hold onto the string. Well, hang on, friend, because you're going to get the quickest start ever to yo-yoing. And your friends and family will be more than a little surprised at how good you get. Ah, yes! This is going to be fun!

I think it would be a lot easier to cut the string.

Getting Started

When you first get a yo-yo, it's tempting to slip your finger into the loop on the end of the string and start yo-yoing. But hold on there, buddy. Unless you're very tall, the string is going to be much too long. Plus, it will be tied with the wrong kind of knot. ("Now why would they do that?" you might ask. Well, most manufacturers figure that if they tied slipknots — pretty hard to do in mass production — they would probably come undone in the shipping process.)

Here's a better way to get started. Let the yo-yo run down the string until it's completely unwound. Hold the yo-yo between your feet on the floor and pull up the string. Following these steps, make a new knot that's even with your belly button.

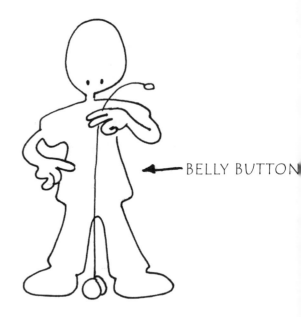

←— BELLY BUTTON

How to Knot your yo-yo:

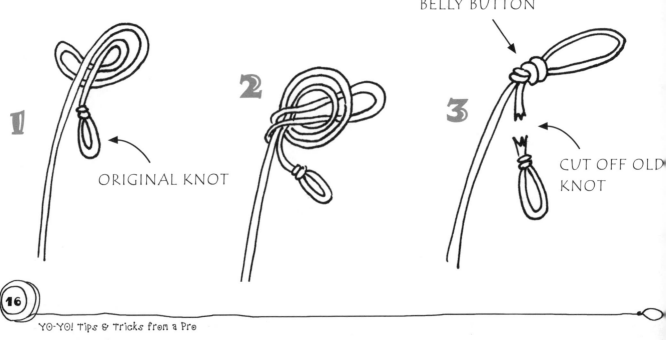

1

ORIGINAL KNOT

2

3

KNOT CLOSE TO BELLY BUTTON

CUT OFF OLD KNOT

Which is Which?

For the purposes of this book, I'll refer to fingers by using the following numbers:

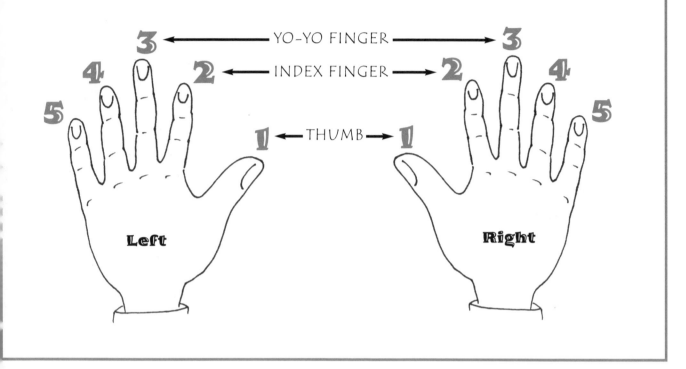

After tying a new knot, make a slipknot for your finger.

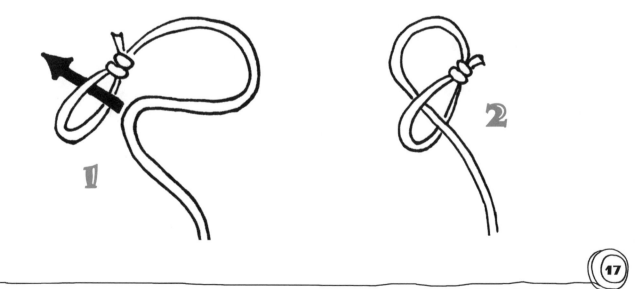

Place the slipknot over your third finger, between the first and second knuckles. All of your tricks will be easier with the string between these two knuckles, closer to your fingernail than to the back of your hand.

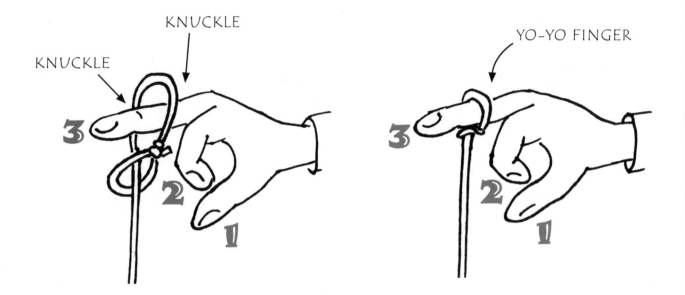

KNUCKLE

KNUCKLE

YO-YO FINGER

Whew! All this work, and you haven't even done a trick yet! It's worth it, though, because now you're set to wind up your yo-yo like a pro!

Quick Starts Tips!™
from a Pro

Righty or Lefty?

Throughout the book, you're going to see the term "opposite hand." I use it to describe the hand you're *not* yo-yoing with (because some people yo-yo with their right hand and some with their left). If you're right-handed, your opposite hand will be your left hand, and if your left-handed, your opposite hand will be your right hand. Duh!

Pat-a-Cake

This is just like playing "pat-a-cake, pat-a-cake" with the yo-yo. Hold the yo-yo in front of you about waist high, with your palm facing down. Open up your hand and let the yo-yo fall. Just as the yo-yo reaches the bottom of the string, gently flick your wrist and hand upward so the yo-yo starts to climb the string. As the yo-yo reaches the top of the string, catch it with your hand.

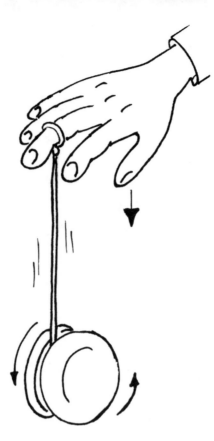

After trying this a few times, try "patting" it back down instead of catching it. As it reaches the bottom of the string, flick your third finger up to make the yo-yo come back up the string. Do this a few times, and then catch the yo-yo in the same hand.

Let me guess: Did you lower your hand to grab it when it came back up? It's tempting, isn't it, but try to wait until the yo-yo comes back up the string. If it doesn't come all the way back, you may want to turn that flick of your finger into a jerk — but not too hard — just enough to get the yo-yo to come back. Keep trying until you get it right. (While you're doing the trick, you can probably even say the rhyme, "Pat-a-cake, pat-a-cake, baker's man. Bake me a cake as fast as you can.") This is the easiest way for everyone to learn to use a yo-yo, and once you have it down, you'll be ready to move on to major fun!

Winding Ways

"What?" you say. "I have to rewind my yo-yo? But I thought it was supposed to return up the string!"

Well, yes, you're right. With practice, that is. When you're first learning, you'll have to rewind when the yo-yo runs out of steam at the end of its string — which, for beginners, is most of the time. (No need to whine, now! It's not exactly the same as running 10 laps around the track! And don't be discouraged. This is quite normal for learners.) For the first thousand hours I was learning, I rewound more than I did anything else. But it didn't take the fun out of practicing and learning. It's all part of the process.

Quick Starts
Jump-Starts!™

Easy Does It: The Hand Wind

It'll take you no time to get the hang of this simple windup. Start by holding the yo-yo in your opposite hand with the tips of your fingers just touching one of the halves (not blocking the string gap). Then, simply wind the string into the gap. It helps to take the string off your finger so the string doesn't twist up.

If the string just spins around and doesn't wind up, place the second finger of your opposite hand over the string gap. On the first wind, wrap the string over your second finger. Then, remove your finger and keep winding.

I've watched some kids try one wrap, and it doesn't work. If this is true for you, too, then try two wraps; that will probably work. If not, go for three. If you're still finding that the string doesn't wind, then it may be time to replace it (see page 12 to find out how).

The Thumb Start

With your yo-yo hand, hold the string of an unwound yo-yo straight up. Place the thumb and third finger of your opposite hand on the string gap of the yo-yo. Hold the string tight with your opposite hand. Quickly slide the thumb down the yo-yo to spin it. This will make the yo-yo wind back up the string a little bit. To get the yo-yo to move up the string, "work" your yo-yo hand (move the yo-yo in an up-and-down motion).

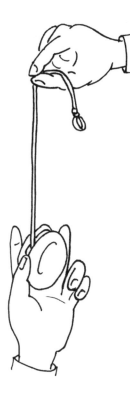

The Choo-Choo Windup

Place the dead yo-yo down on the floor standing on its edges. Stretch the string out in a straight line without knocking over the yo-yo. Give a slight tug with your third finger to get the "choo-choo" rolling toward you. As the yo-yo begins to roll, move your hand along the floor so the yo-yo can roll right to the "station" (your hand).

21

The Two-Finger Start

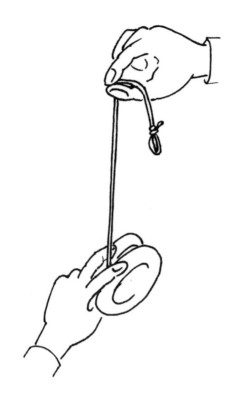

Place the second and third fingers of your opposite hand on the yo-yo on either side of the gap, with the bottom of the yo-yo resting lightly on your thumb and the last two fingers. Like you did with the thumb start, hold the string of an unwound yo-yo straight up with your yo-yo hand. Hold the string tight with your opposite hand. Quickly slide the two fingers of your opposite hand down the yo-yo to spin it up the string a bit. Work your yo-yo hand to get the yo-yo to move up the string.

The Kick Start

No, you don't kick the yo-yo to get it going! For this windup, place the dead yo-yo on the floor in front of you. Gently put the toe of your shoe on the yo-yo with the toe just touching the string. Hold the string tight with your yo-yo hand and snap your toe off the yo-yo down to the floor. The yo-yo will spin up the string. Work your yo-yo hand up and down to get the yo-yo moving. (P.S. This is one windup method that looks really cool if you can get the hang of it!)

Yes!

No!

Walking the Plank

Place the yo-yo between the thumb and second finger of your yo-yo hand, with the string still attached to the third finger and coming off the top of the yo-yo. With the fingers of your opposite hand, grab the string that's hanging down. Raise the opposite hand higher than the yo-yo hand.

Place the string gap on the string and release the yo-yo from between your thumb and second finger. As the yo-yo balances on the string, slowly lift the yo-yo hand and lower the opposite hand. Make sure the yo-yo moves *slowly* along the string so it winds up the string and doesn't just slide along the string.

When the yo-yo reaches the opposite hand, pick it up with your thumb and second finger and gently drop it down in front of you. Work your yo-yo hand up and down to get the yo-yo moving up the string.

This trick is a great way to impress your friends and family! It looks so flashy, when all you're really doing is rolling up the yo-yo. Take a bow!

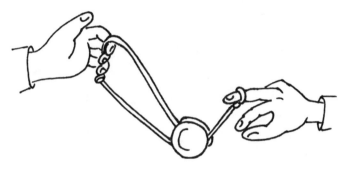

So there you have it — the windup tricks and beginning techniques that have you on your way to becoming a yo-yo whiz! Now, ready for some real fun?

Quick Starts Tips!™ from a Pro

Why Won't My Yo-Yo Return?

If your yo-yo keeps sleeping and won't return, the string may be too loose. Not to worry! Check the tip on tightening the string (page 14).

Another reason why the yo-yo won't return may be that the string is worn out, frayed, or knotted. If this is the case, sounds like it's time for a little string maintenance (pages 11–14).

SOLO YO-YO

Remember in *The Wizard of Oz* when someone tells Dorothy before she starts out on the Yellow Brick Road, "It's always best to start at the beginning"? (Give yourself 10 points if you can remember *who* said it to her!)

In yo-yoing, two moves in particular — the *Gravity Pull* (page 25) and the *Sleeper* (page 26) — could be considered the beginning since most of the tricks you'll learn later start with one of these. Practice them until you feel really comfortable with them, and they'll take you as far as you want to go. On the way, instead of lions, tigers, bears (or even flying monkeys — oh, wait a minute; there *are* monkeys later on!), you'll come across such fantastic tricks as the *Creeper* (page 28), the *UFO* (page 36), the *Cowboy* (page 31), and many others.

So, let's start at the beginning!

Not a very good Forward Pass catch.

Time for Tricks!
Gravity Pull

Gravity — it's not just a good idea; it's the law (as any science fan will tell you). But this trick lets you defy the laws of gravity! Some people will be able to do this trick the first time, but the rest of us may need to practice so the yo-yo won't wobble sideways and throw off other tricks. Don't get discouraged; practice makes progress!

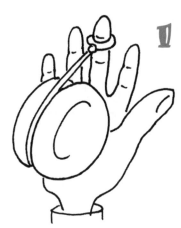

1

Hold arm out in front, with palm facing up and string coming off top of finger.

2

Place fingers on yo-yo with third finger on groove.

3

Bend arm up, with the yo-yo at ear level, as if showing off a big muscle.

4

Flick your wrist and throw the yo-yo straight down.

Keep your palm facing up for steps 1 to 4. Once the yo-yo has completely left your hand and is traveling down the string, turn your hand over so the palm is facing down. As the yo-yo reaches the bottom of the string, give the string a slight tug upward with the third finger. This will cause the yo-yo to travel back up the string. You'll know you've got it when the yo-yo returns so quickly that it slaps your hand!

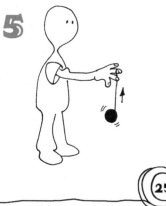

5

Solo Yo-Yo

Sleeper

The trick to the *Sleeper* is in getting your yo-yo to sleep for increasing periods of time. At first, it may sleep for only a few seconds. With practice, you'll be able to get it to sleep from 8 to 10 seconds, which is enough time to do lots of sleeping tricks.

Start the *Sleeper* the same way you started the *Gravity Pull* (page 25): Hold your arm out in front of you with your palm facing up and the string coming off the top of the yo-yo. Make your "buff" muscle again so the yo-yo is at ear level. Then, flick your wrist as you throw the yo-yo down and out in front of you about 3' (90 cm) at a 45° angle. Don't turn your palm over yet. If you turn it over too soon, the yo-yo will wobble sideways.

Stop your arm at about waist level, and relax your hand and wrist to allow the string a little "give." The yo-yo should be "sleeping" at the end of the string. Now turn your hand over so your palm faces down. Give a sharp tug with your third finger so the yo-yo will return to your hand. With practice, you'll be able to feel when the yo-yo is running out of steam and needs to be snapped back.

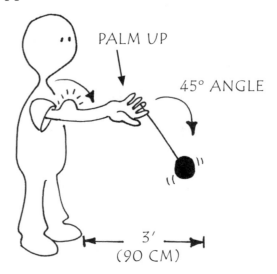

PALM UP

45° ANGLE

3'
(90 CM)

Champion Challenge!

Dueling Sleepers

Gather some yo-yo buddies and all start a *Sleeper* at the same time. The first person whose *Sleeper* stops can step aside while the others begin again, until you get down to two and then a winner.

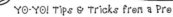

WHAT'S THE DIFF?

Do the *Gravity Pull* (page 25) and the *Sleeper* (page 26) feel pretty much the same to you? They do to lots of yo-yoers, but there are some noticeable differences. When you throw a *Sleeper*, the yo-yo spins at the end of the string (or is supposed to), but in the *Gravity Pull*, the yo-yo goes down and back up without sleeping. Another difference is that the *Sleeper* is thrown at a 45° angle to get it to stop close in front of you. If you throw it straight down — the same way you throw a *Gravity Pull* — it will swing in back of you. Throwing it at an angle makes it come to a good stopping place in preparation for other moves.

Walk the Dog

This is probably the most famous trick, the one everyone will ask you to do! The only thing you need is a firm surface to perform on because the trick won't work on a soft rug.

Start by throwing a hard, fast *Sleeper* (page 26). (Don't throw it straight into the floor or you'll be walking a broken yo-yo.) Gently lower the yo-yo to barely touch the floor so the yo-yo rolls forward like a playful puppy. Let the spinning motion gently "walk the dog" out in front of you. (Never walk your dog on driveways or sidewalks, or your yo-yo will look like it got into a dog fight.) Give the string a tug, and the yo-yo will return to your hand.

Finishing Touches...

If you want to walk your dog a little longer, walk slowly behind it. (But don't walk it too far or your dog will get tired and stop moving.) Whistle and give your "leash" a tug; then watch your dog come right back home.

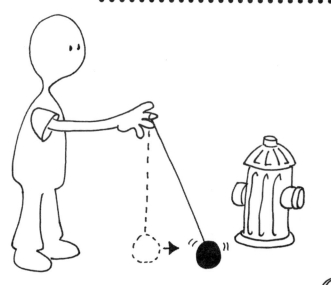

Solo Yo-Yo

Creeper

This trick is similar to *Walk the Dog* (page 27). Throw a hard, fast *Sleeper* (page 26) and "walk" the yo-yo out in front of you. Bend down on one knee and lower the string to the floor. Let the yo-yo sleep for a few seconds. With your hand on the floor, palm facing up, give the string a slight tug, and the yo-yo will creep along the floor back to your hand. You can also whistle and say, "Here, boy," and your doggie will come right back to you!

Quick Starts
Jump-Starts!™

What If My Yo-Yo Won't Sleep?

If your yo-yo won't sleep, check to make sure there are no knots or kinks in the string (see Spaghetti String and Taking Out Knots, pages 12 and 14).

If the string is all right and it still won't sleep, then it's probably too tight (see page 14 for loosening tips).

✱ Do a little string maintenance, and then try the *Sleeper* (page 26). If the yo-yo still won't sleep, give it a few more spins clockwise to get it to work (or counterclockwise if you think you've twisted it *too* tight).

✱ Are you still having trouble? If so, try throwing a little harder. Check that you're throwing the yo-yo straight, that it doesn't lean to one side or the other.

✱ Another way to practice is to throw the yo-yo out in front of you. Place an unbreakable object (like a pillow) about 4' (120 cm) in front of you, and aim the yo-yo toward that object without hitting it.

YO-YO! Tips & Tricks from a Pro

from a Pro

Way Cool Yo-Yo Dude!

To make the *Forward Pass* look effortless, try not to throw the yo-yo too hard. The harder you throw it, the faster it will end up right back in your hand. A gentle throw will give the trick a nonchalant air that'll make you look as if you weren't even trying!

Forward Pass

Hold the yo-yo in your hand as if you were going to do a *Sleeper* (page 26). Instead of making a muscle, place your arm down by your side with the knuckles facing down and the back of your hand facing forward. Swing your arm forward and flick your wrist to throw the yo–yo straight out in front of you. When it reaches the end of the string, turn your hand so your palm faces up and catch the yo-yo when it returns to you.

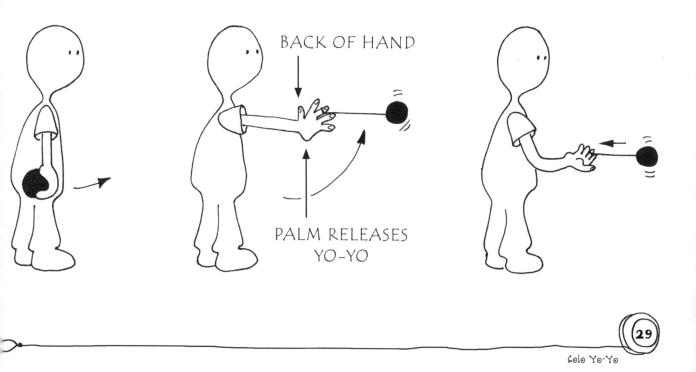

BACK OF HAND

PALM RELEASES
YO-YO

Around the World

Okay, here we go! It's show (or is that show-off) time! Never mind; when you're good, you're very good!

Throw a hard *Forward Pass* (page 29). Once the yo-yo is at the end of the string, swing it in a full circle on the side of your body, up over your head, down behind you, and up in front of you. (Very little hand or arm movement is needed to swing the yo-yo in an orbit on the side of your body; it's mostly in the wrist action.) When the yo-yo has completed a full orbit, give the string a jerk and watch the yo-yo return home from its travels. Wow!

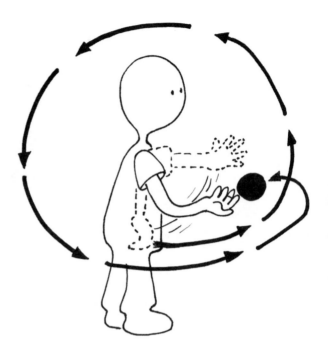

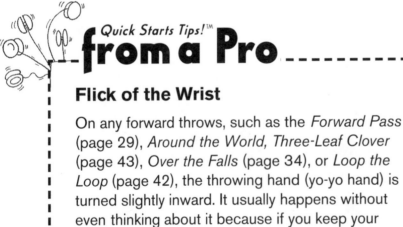

Quick Starts Tips!™
from a Pro

Flick of the Wrist

On any forward throws, such as the *Forward Pass* (page 29), *Around the World*, *Three-Leaf Clover* (page 43), *Over the Falls* (page 34), or *Loop the Loop* (page 42), the throwing hand (yo-yo hand) is turned slightly inward. It usually happens without even thinking about it because if you keep your hand stiff with the palm facing down, the string will get all tangled around your hand or fingers or the yo-yo will smack into your hand.

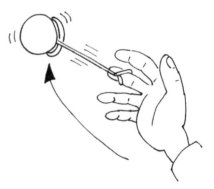

YO-YO! Tips & Tricks from a Pro

Finishing Touches ....

As you get better with *Around the World*, you can try two or more "trips" in front of you by continuing to swing your yo-yo in full circles. Try orbiting backward, too. And sound effects always work: How about an airplane or a blastoff noise?

Cowboy

Cowboy is similar to *Around the World* (page 30), except that it's done over your head to look like a lasso. Throw a *Sleeper* (page 26) to the side toward your opposite shoulder. Swing it over your head. When it comes around, give the string a tug so the yo-yo returns to your hand. Try doing it several times over your head. Instead of an airplane noise, how about "YAHOO!"

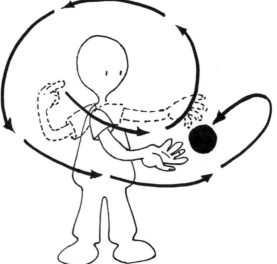

Solo Yo-Yo

Around the Corner

Throw a hard, fast *Sleeper* (page 26). Turn your hand so your palm is facing forward; then, raise your hand to shoulder height. Swing the yo-yo out to the side and then behind your arm. Position the string between your elbow and shoulder. Hold your hand up as if you were saying, "Stop!" or waving good-bye. Flick your fingers forward. The yo-yo will jump over your shoulder and fall down in front of you. Give the string a slight tug so the yo-yo snaps back to your hand.

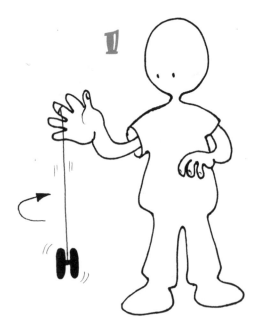

YO-YO! Tips & Tricks from a Pro

Quick Starts Tips!™
from a Pro

Whoa, Yo-Yo!

Around the World (page 30), *Cowboy* (page 31), and *Around the Corner* are very easy tricks to do, but they can be dangerous. Make sure you have a lot of room in front of you, behind you, and over your head — at least 5' (150 cm). Check to see if the string is old, worn, or frayed. Don't do the trick if there is someone in front or in back of you, or if there are breakable items around like lamps, windows, TVs, or your little brother or sister.

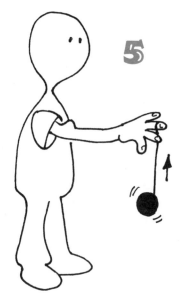

5

4

STOP!

Champion Challenge!

Skeet Shooting

Ask a friend to throw a paper or Styrofoam cup into the air, while you try to shoot it out of the air with a *Forward Pass*.

Over the Falls

Throw a *Forward Pass* (page 29). When the yo-yo reaches the end of its string and starts its return flight, don't turn your hand over to catch it. Keep it in the same throwing position (with your palm down).

Just before it reaches your hand, flick your wrist in a counterclockwise motion and loop the yo-yo over the inside of your hand; then, let it drop straight down, "over the falls." When the yo-yo reaches the end of the string, give it a slight tug to return it to your hand.

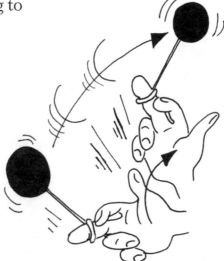

YO-YO! Tips & Tricks from a Pro

Hop the Fence

Throw a *Gravity Pull* (page 25). As the yo-yo comes back, let it come up over the top of your hand by flicking your wrist to "hop" the yo-yo over the "fence" (your hand).

The yo-yo will continue down to the floor. When the yo-yo reaches the end of the string, give a slight tug so the yo-yo returns to your hand. As you get better with this trick, you can try two or more "hops" without stopping.

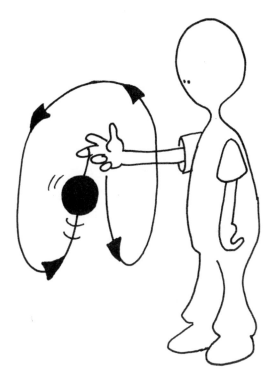

Finishing Touches •••••••••••••••••••••

Another version of this is to throw a *Gravity Pull* (page 25), but this time, instead of looping the yo-yo to the inside of your hand, loop it over the outside of your hand. Now, double your fun by alternating inside and outside loops!

UFO

aka (also known as) Sleeping Beauty and Flying Saucer

This is a great trick to watch, and it's a great way to adjust the tension of the yo-yo string. (If you throw to the right, it will tighten the string. If you throw to the left, it will loosen the string.)

Throw a *Sleeper* (page 26) across your body at a 45° angle. Your yo-yo will spin sideways, resembling a "flying saucer." Reach down with the opposite hand and pinch the yo-yo string 4"–5" (10–12.5 cm) from the yo-yo. Lift up the string until both hands are at the same height. Give the pinched string a gentle tug and throw up both hands. The yo-yo will wind up on its side and return to your hand.

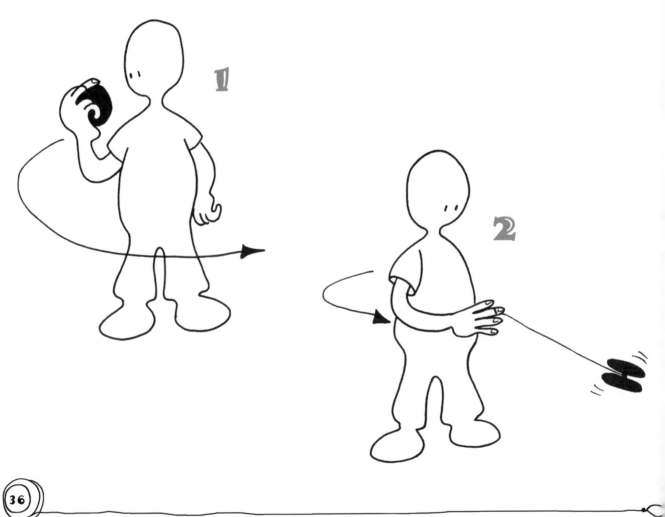

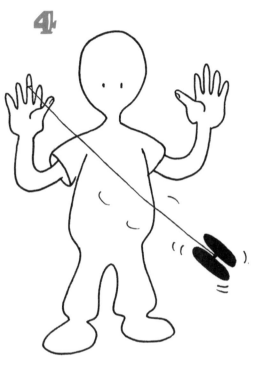

from a Pro

The Hand Is Faster Than the Eye!

The UFO is a great trick to create the illusion that you know lots of different tricks. See if you can fool your audience! Announce that you're going to throw a *UFO*, do the trick, and then do another trick or two. Tell them you're going to throw a *Sleeping Beauty*, do the trick, and then another trick or two after it. Next, announce your *Flying Saucer* and do the trick, followed by a different trick or two. Did anyone notice that the three were all the same trick?

DYNAMO YO-YO

Hey, you've come a long way! Feels pretty good, doesn't it? Now that you've mastered some of the easier tricks, let's try some more yo-yo challenges. These aren't *real* difficult; they just require a little practice. In no time at all, you'll be fascinating all your friends and family with a solid yo-yo repertoire.

Can you make your yo-yo sleep?

Fantastic Feats!

Breakaway

The *Breakaway* uses the same motions as the *Sleeper* (page 26), except it's thrown off to the side instead of down in front of you. This is a good one to practice because it's the starting action for a lot of trickier tricks you'll be able to learn down the road.

Hold the yo-yo as if you were going to throw a *Sleeper* (page 26), but instead of flexing your muscle in front of you, flex it to your outer side. Throw the yo-yo off the same side, about shoulder height.

When the yo-yo reaches the end of the string, relax your hand slightly, but keep your elbow bent. The yo-yo will swing down and make a half circle in front of you. When it reaches the opposite side, give it a slight tug so it returns to your hand.

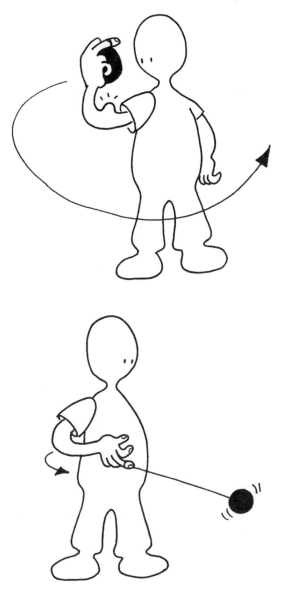

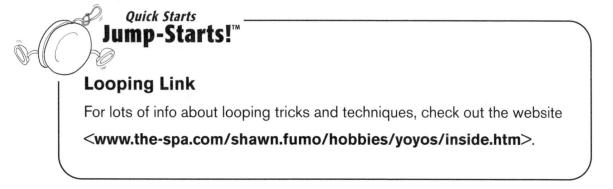

Quick Starts
Jump-Starts!™

Looping Link

For lots of info about looping tricks and techniques, check out the website <**www.the-spa.com/shawn.fumo/hobbies/yoyos/inside.htm**>.

Dynamo Yo-Yo

Rock the Baby

Another popular trick, *Rock the Baby* is one of the few you can *practice* with a dead yo-yo, even though when you do the trick, you'll want your yo-yo to be sleeping. To practice, let the yo-yo hang down in front of you, with your yo-yo hand about eye level.

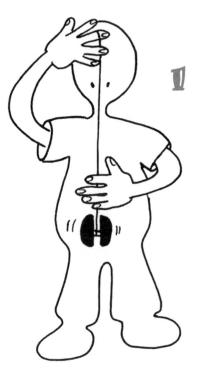

Place the *palm* of the opposite hand against the string about halfway down, with your fingers spread wide. (The string should be between your body and your hand.) With your opposite hand, push the string *toward* you.

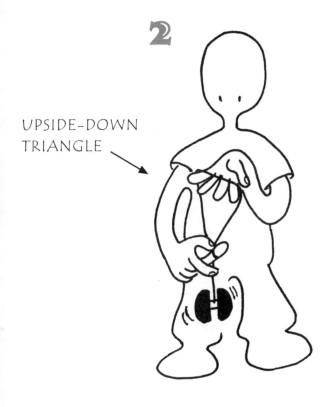

UPSIDE-DOWN TRIANGLE

To form the upside-down triangle, move the yo-yo hand *away from* you, in an arc over the opposite hand, and pinch the string with your thumb and second finger about 5" (12.5 cm) from the yo-yo. (Let the string rotate around your finger naturally as you move your hand around.) This will form an upside-down triangle with the string.

Raise the yo-yo hand as you lower the opposite hand, turning it so your palm faces down. You should end up with a right-side-up triangle. Spread the fingers of your bottom hand and make the string ride close to the fingernails of your thumb and little finger. This will form a good base for your triangle. "Rock the baby" gently in its cradle.

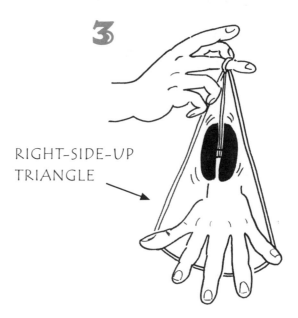

RIGHT-SIDE-UP
TRIANGLE

Practice these motions with a dead yo-yo until you can do them without thinking. Once you have them down, start off with a fast, hard *Sleeper* (page 26), followed by steps 1 through 3. Now you can rock that sleeping baby and hum it a lullaby.

When you finish *Rocking the Baby*, drop the pinched string. If your yo-yo is still sleeping, it will snap back up the string and return to your hand.

Dynamo Yo-Yo

Loop the Loop

(Hey, didn't I ride this at the amusement park?)

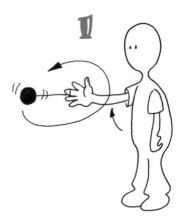

Wow, you're getting very good. If you've gotten this far, you're ready for this challenging trick. It takes a lot of practice, so don't get discouraged. It's fun to learn because it enables you to do lots of other tricks. So here we go on the *Loop the Loop*.

To start, throw a *Forward Pass* (page 29) and then turn your hand slightly so your palm is facing inward.

Instead of catching the yo-yo on its return, wait until it's about 6" (15 cm) from your hand.

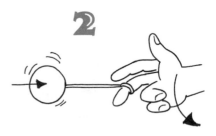

Then, flick your wrist in a counterclockwise motion to send it back out again.

Catch the yo-yo on its return.

Finishing Touches ......

As you improve with this trick, try to add more loops without stopping. After you've mastered many loops, try doing it with your other hand. When you get real good with the opposite hand, try doing loops with both hands. You'll look like a real pro! (Just remember: Right-handed loops will loosen the string one half-turn. Left-handed loops will tighten it one half-turn.)

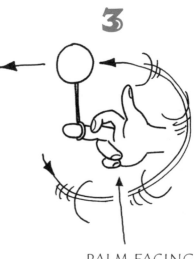

PALM FACING
INWARD

Three-Leaf Clover

If you enjoyed learning *Loop the Loop* (page 42), then you're in for a treat with this variation.

Throw a *Loop the Loop* at a 45° angle upward in front of you. When the yo-yo comes back toward your hand, don't catch it. Flick your wrist in a counterclockwise motion to direct it out in a normal *Loop the Loop*. When it returns this time, flick your wrist again in a counterclockwise motion, but aim the yo-yo in a downward path, straight down your leg like an *Over the Falls* (page 34). Catch the yo-yo as it returns to your hand.

That's your *Three-Leaf Clover*. Try singing, "I'm looking over a four-leaf clover that I overlooked before ..." (See if someone you know knows the tune.) People will be so amazed at your yo-yo talent that they won't even notice it's only a three-leaf clover!

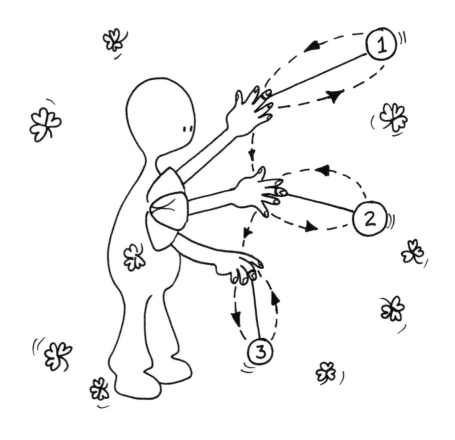

Champion Challenge!

Getting Loopy!

Gather a bunch of your yo-yoing friends to see who can do a *Loop the Loop* for the longest time.

Champion Challenge!

Ambidextrous Amateur

Can you yo-yo with one hand and play paddle ball with the other? See how many other things you can do with the opposite hand while you yo-yo.

Shoot the Moon

Here's another variation of *Loop the Loop* (page 42). To start, throw the first *Loop the Loop* straight out in front of you. When it returns, don't catch it. Flick your wrist in a counterclockwise motion, directing it upward at a 45° angle. This is when your yo-yo will "shoot the moon." Catch the yo-yo as it returns to your hand.

Elevator

Start with a hard *Sleeper* (page 26). Take the third finger of your opposite hand and push it against the string so that the yo-yo hangs from the third finger. Now lower your yo-yo hand and raise your opposite hand. When the yo-yo is about 2" (5 cm) above your yo-yo hand, move your yo-yo hand forward so the yo-yo slips onto the string.

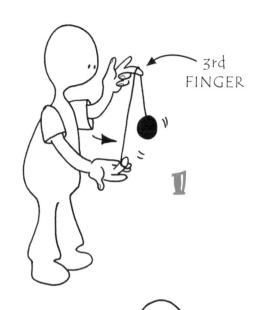

3RD FINGER

1

Pull up the third finger of your opposite hand while you pull down your yo-yo hand. This will make the "elevator" slide up the string.

2

3

4

When the yo-yo is about 2" (5 cm) from your opposite hand, flick your wrist; the yo-yo will jump off the string before it winds back down the string.

45

Try, Try Again!

What if your yo-yo runs out of steam? What if you get tangled up like a kitten in a whirl of yarn? What if your yo-yo goes bonkers — *for real* — and hits you on the arm or gets caught on your clothes? Well . . . it happens to the best of us! And when it happens to me, I do what everyone else does — rewind and start again. When a trick doesn't work, don't get discouraged. You can learn something from each mistake you make!

Quick Starts Tips!™
from a Pro

Loosey-Goosey or Tight as a Fist

As you probably know by now, string tension can make a difference between a great sleeper and a not-so-interesting yawner. Not only can certain tricks loosen or tighten your string, but so can the hand you perform them with. For example, a *Loop the Loop* (page 42) done with the right hand tends to tighten the yo-yo string; done with the left hand, it tends to loosen the string. (Now how in the world does that happen?)

As a rule, right-handed yo-yoers will mostly need to loosen their strings after playing for a while. Left-handed spinners will often have to tighten their strings.

But this is not *a hard and fast* rule. There are lots of factors that affect how quickly your string might become too tight or too loose: how many times you've thrown each trick, how correctly the yo-yo moved, the force of the throw, etc. As you familiarize yourself with many different tricks, you can alternate string-tightening tricks with string-loosening tricks, but in the beginning, one rule is all you need: If you've done some tricks that tightened the string and the yo-yo isn't working properly, you'll have to loosen the string. If you've done some tricks that loosened the string and the yo-yo isn't working properly, you'll have to tighten the string.

Monkey on a String

Monkey on a String is the same as the *Elevator* (page 45), but it happens in reverse. Starting with a hard *Sleeper* (page 26), place the third finger of your opposite hand against the string just below your yo-yo hand. The third finger should be on the *outside* of the string, pushing the string toward your body. Then, follow the same directions as the *Elevator*. Make noises like a monkey. If you can't make monkey noises, make banana noises!

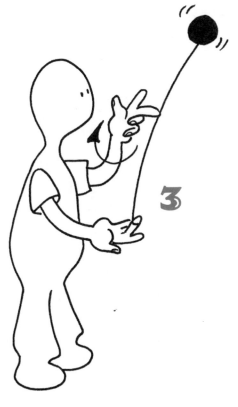

Dynamo Yo-Yo

Flying Trapeze

Throw a *Breakaway* (page 39) so the yo-yo swings in an arc in front of you. Your opposite hand should be waist-high, with the second finger pointing forward. As the yo-yo swings up to your opposite hand, stop the string with your outstretched second finger about 4"–5" (10–12.5 cm) from the yo-yo. The yo-yo's momentum will cause it to swing over your finger.

Now the fun part — as the yo-yo swings over your finger, let it land with its axle on the string. (Picture the yo-yo jumping up and landing on a balance beam.) It takes some practice, but it's a blast when you finally get it!

As you move your hands closer together, the man will swing on the flying trapeze. Hum or sing, "He flew through the air with the greatest of ease. The daring young man on the flying trapeze." If you pull your hands apart quickly, you'll flip the daring young man on the flying trapeze right into the air. Remove your second finger as soon as you flip the yo-yo, and it will return to your yo-yoing hand. Ta-da!

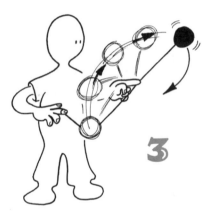

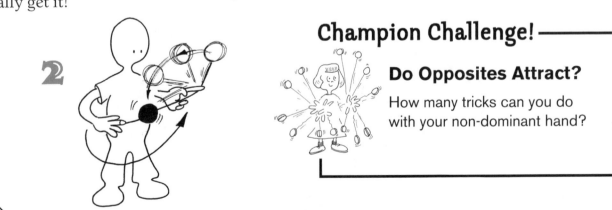

Champion Challenge!

Do Opposites Attract?

How many tricks can you do with your non-dominant hand?

HO-HO YO-YO

By now, you've gotten pretty far with your solo and dynamo yo-yo tricks. Congratulations! Give yourself a pat on the back. You must really enjoy yo-yo tricks to have learned so much. And the exciting thing is that there's always room to learn more. For every yo-yo pro out there, a new trick is being developed at this very moment. That's right: Yo-yoers just like you develop new tricks. So, why not have some fun and develop some original tricks? And why not slip in a few laughs between your amazing yo-yo tricks? A few of the following ho-ho yo-yo tricks are sure to get some giggles!

That's a good trick. Can you do it again?

More Yo-Yo Fun!

Jumping the Dog Through a Hoop

Throw a fast *Sleeper* (page 26). Lower the yo-yo to the floor as though you were about to *Walk the Dog* (page 27), only start it *behind* you.

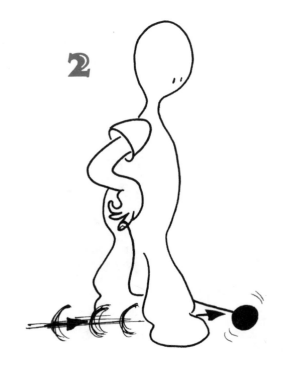

Move one leg to the other side of the yo-yo and *Walk the Dog* between your legs. Place your yo-yo hand close to your hip to form the "hoop."

When your "dog" reaches the end of its leash, give it a slight tug so it jumps right back through your legs and down in front of you. Give the leash another slight tug, and the dog will return to your hand (or get all tangled up, as pesky dogs often do!).

3

Dog Bite

Keep your feet about 2' (60 cm) apart and throw a hard, fast *Sleeper* (page 26). Swing the yo-yo between your legs. Give a tug on the string as you move your leg on the yo-yo side so the "dog" will "bite" your pants. (I hate when that happens!) It helps if you have on baggy pants — unless, of course, you have baggy legs.

Champion Challenge!

What a Drag!

How about a drag race with your yo-yo? Line up with some yo-yoing friends to sleep your yo-yos. Have everyone pull her yo-yo off her finger and let it rip across the floor. The yo-yo that goes the farthest or the first one over a finish line is the winner.

Slurping Spaghetti

Throw a fast *Sleeper* (page 26). Reach down with your opposite hand and pinch the string about 2"–3" (5–7.5 cm) from the topage Bring this up and place it in the thumb and second finger of your yo-yo hand to form a loop. Make a few more loops by doing this two or three times.

Move the yo-yo hand up toward your mouth with your palm facing down, holding the "spaghetti." Make loud slurping noises as you let go of the string. You'll get plenty of laughs as the spaghetti looks as if it's being sucked into your mouth. Take a bow as you pretend to wipe your face with a napkin.

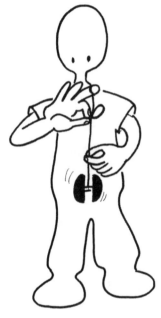

Snapping Spaghetti

While you're "slurping spaghetti," make sure when you raise your yo-yo so that your hand is between the yo-yo and your mouth. And take special care not to move your yo-yo hand. Otherwise, the yo-yo won't go down to the end of the string, but will quickly snap back toward your face. Ouch! That's when you'll be glad you put your yo-yo hand between your mouth and the yo-yo!

Runaway Dog

Throw a fast *Sleeper* (page 26). Remove the string from your finger and lower the yo-yo to the floor to *Walk the Dog* (page 27). As the "dog" is walking, release the string and it will run up the street. *Dog gone!*

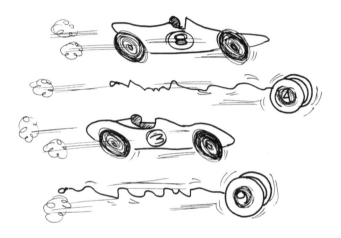

Dragster

The *Dragster* is the same as the *Runaway Dog, except* for the addition of sound effects; as it runs off, make loud screeching tire sounds.

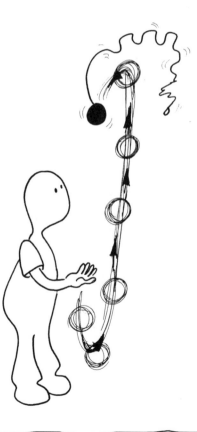

Skyrocket

This one is similar to *Runaway Dog* and *Dragster*, but it's more dramatic. Throw a fast *Sleeper* (page 26) and take the string off your finger. Don't let go of the string yet. Give the string a slight tug to get the yo-yo to start returning up the string. Before the yo-yo reaches your hand, let go of the string and pull your hand out of the way. The yo-yo will rocket up into the air. Catch it as it comes back to earth.

Ho-Ho Yo-Yo

Buzz Saw

aka **Rattlesnake, Walk the Duck, and Shoe Shine**

What a difference a few sound effects make! These are all basically the same trick with different names. Throw a fast *Sleeper* (page 26). Set the yo-yo down on a piece of paper or cardboard to make different sounds like a buzz saw or rattlesnake. Do it in a water puddle or pan of water for *Walk the Duck*. Do a *Sleeper* on your shoe for *Shoe Shine*.

Now try doing a *Sleeper* on different materials like tin, plastic, or wood. What kinds of sounds and names can you come up with?

Finishing Touches . . . . .

For some real pizzazz, practice catching the *Skyrocket* in a pocket!

So very cool!

Champion Challenge!

Something New under the Sun

Start with a *Sleeper* (page 26) or a *Forward Pass* (page 29). See what kinds of tricks you and your friends can create. Then, hold a competition to see whose new trick wows your friends the most!

Oops!

Dings in the Ceiling

Tricks like the *Skyrocket* (page 53) are best done outdoors because a fast-moving yo-yo really does seem to reach the sky. Also, if you miss it when it comes down, you won't ruin your yo-yo when it lands on the grass.

Walk the Cat

Hmmm… I'll bet you're wondering how this trick might be different from *Walk the Dog* (page 27). Give up? You have to start with an *upside-down Sleeper* (page 26)! It's a little difficult at first, but keep at it because this is a fun one.

Hold the yo-yo in your hand as if you were going to throw a *Sleeper*, but instead of the string coming off the top, hold it so the string comes off the bottom.

It'll probably feel weird when you first try it because this isn't a natural position for throwing the yo-yo, so it's likely to spin crookedly. Rely on your stick-to-itiveness until you can throw the yo-yo straight instead of sideways for this trick.

Once you've perfected the throw, lower the yo-yo gently to the floor as if you were going to *Walk the Dog.* Your audience will expect the "cat" to walk in front of you, but you know how independent a cat is! This one will shoot backward. Then, you can either walk backward with it or act as if the cat is dragging you backward. Now who's walking whom?

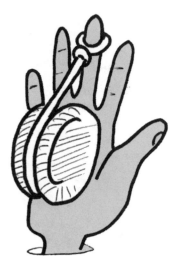

Nope!

Yep!

Quick Starts Tips!™
from a Pro

More Tricks to Try

Check out the following websites for more yo-yo fun!

Ken's World on a String **<http://199.44.235.54/tricks.html>**

Cosmic Yo-Yo Tricks **<www.iwc.com/cosmicyo/trickindex.html>**

YO mania.com Yo-Yo Tricks and Tips! **<www.yomania.com/tricks.htm>**

(See Resources, page 60, for websites about the world of yo-yoing.)

Skin the Cat

aka Tidal Wave

Throw a fast *Sleeper* (page 26). Place the second finger of your opposite hand under your yo-yo finger. Lift your second finger out and upward, while you lower your yo-yo hand. When the yo-yo is 4"–5" (10–12.5 cm) from your opposite hand, flip it up with your second finger and tug gently with your yo-yo hand. As the yo-yo comes back toward your opposite hand, don't catch it. Let it swing over your hand and flick it back out into a *Forward Pass* (page 29).

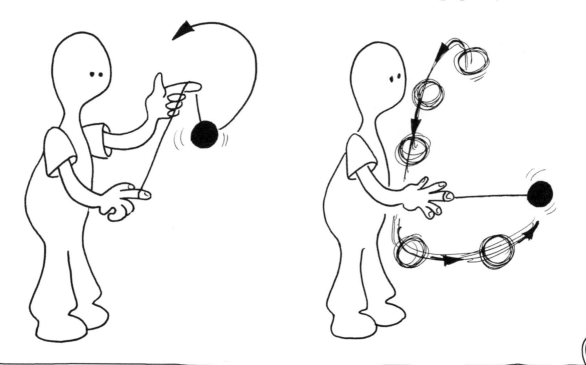

Playing the Bass

Throw a *Sleeper* (page 26), but don't let it touch the floor. Pluck the string as if you were playing a bass fiddle. Don't forget those *"Dump, dump, pa, dump"* sounds.

Bow and Arrow

Throw a fast *Sleeper* (page 26). With the second finger of your opposite hand, pull the string between your finger and thumb like you are pulling a bow. When the yo-yo is 2"–3" (5–7.5 cm) from your thumb, release the string. The yo-yo will snap back to your hand.

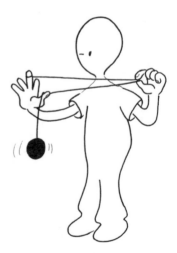

Champion Challenge!

Yo-Yo Talent Show

Want a great routine for the next talent show at school? Find a yo-yo friend and develop a back-to-back routine (with your sides facing the audience) doing *synchronized* tricks (the same tricks at the same time). If one of you is left-handed and the other is right-handed, even better! One of you can call out the names of the tricks: "*Forward Pass, Shoot the Moon, Hop the Fence, Elevator, Three-Leaf Clover* ...."

The secret is doing tricks that require the yo-yo to be in front of you both. That way you can keep your backs to each other so that you look like mirror images!

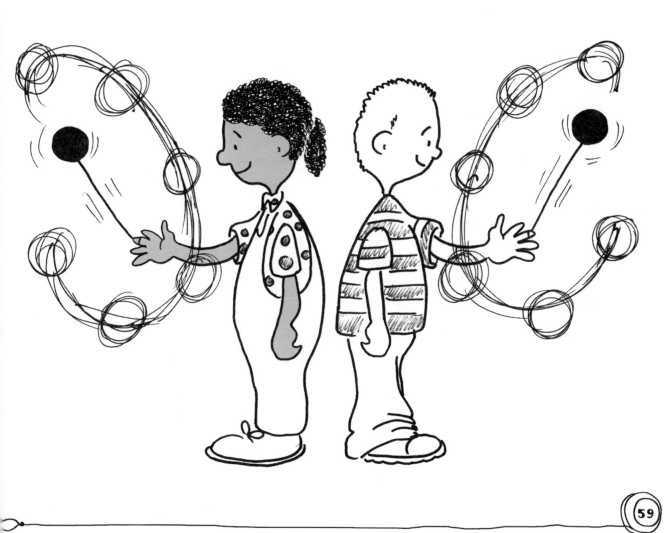

Yo-Yo Resources

Yo-Yos on the WWW:

The American Yo-Yo Association
<**www.pd.net/yoyo**>

Duncan Toys
<**www.duncan-toys.com**>

Playmaxx
<**www.proyo.com**>

Yomega
<**www.yomega.com**>

The Yo-Yo Man
<**www.smothersbrothers.com/yoyoman.html**>

Infinite Illusions
<**www.yoyoguy.com**>

Cosmic Yo-Yos
<**http://wc.com/cosmicyo/**>

Bob's Land of Yo
<**www.intergate.bc.ca/personal/bobb/
yo.html**>

Good Yo-Yo Links
<**http://yoyoing.com**>

Yo-Yo Newsletters:

Noble Disk
<**www.cybertours.com/nobledisk**>
124 Cabot St.
Portsmouth NH 03801

Yo-Yo Times
<**www.yoyotimes.com**>
P.O. Box 1519 - WB
Herndon, VA 20172
(703) 715-6187

Yo-Yo String:

Duncan Toys
(all cotton fiber, packs of 5 strings)
P.O. Box 5
Middlefield, OH 44062
(800) 232-3474

Yomega
(all cotton fiber, packs of 5 strings)
P.O. Box 4146
Fall River, MA 02723
(800) 338-8796

Infinite String
(all cotton fiber, packs of 10, 100, or 1,000
   strings!)
P.O. Box 2584
Tallahassee, FL 32316
(800) yoyo guy (969-6489)

Videos and Books:

Available at all bookstores and toy stores
that sell yo-yos.

Index

A
Around the Corner, 32, 33
Around the World, 30, 33
axles, 8–9

B
Bow and Arrow, 58
Breakaway, 39
butterfly yo-yo shape, 8
Buzz Saw (aka Rattlesnake, Walk
   the Duck, Shoe Shine), 54

C
centrifugal clutch yo-yo, 9
Champion Challenge!, 26, 33, 43,
   44, 48, 51, 55, 59
Choo-Choo Windup, 21
Cowboy, 31, 33
Creeper, 28

D
dead yo-yo, defined, 6
dismountable (take apart) yo-yo, 9
Dog Bite, 51
Dragster, 53

E
Elevator, 45, 59

F
fingers, numbering, 17
fixed axle yo-yo, 9
Flying Saucer, 36–37
Flying Trapeze, 48
Forward Pass, 29, 30, 33, 55, 59

G
getting started, 16–23
Gravity Pull, 25, 27, 35

H
Hand Wind, 20
Hop the Fence, 35, 59

J
Jumping the Dog Through a
   Hoop, 50

K
Kick Start, 22
knots, 14, 16–18, 28

L
Loop the Loop, 30, 42, 43, 46

M
Monkey on a String, 47

N
newsletters, 60

O
Over the Falls, 30, 34
Oops!, 12, 46, 52, 55
opposite hand, defined, 18

P
parts of a yo-yo, 8
Pat-a-Cake, 19
plastic yo-yos, 5
Playing the Bass, 58

Q
questions about yo-yos,
   answered, 5–6
Quick Starts Tips!™ from a Pro,
   5, 9, 14, 18, 23, 29, 30, 33,
   37, 46, 57
Quick Starts Jump-Starts!™,
   20, 28, 39

R
Rattlesnake, 54
records, yo-yo, 6
Rock the Baby, 40
Runaway Dog, 53

S
Shoe Shine, 54
Shoot the Moon, 44
Skin the Cat (aka Tidal Wave), 57
Skyrocket, 53, 55
Sleeper, 26, 27, 28, 54, 55
Sleeping Beauty, 36–37
sleeping yo-yo
   defined, 6
   dueling, 26

slimline yo-yo shape, 8
slipknot, 17–18
Slurping Spaghetti, 52
space shuttle *Atlantis*, yo-yos on, 7
string, 11–14, 23, 28, 60
   changing, 12–13
   knots in, removing, 14, 16
   length of, 16
   sources for, 60
   tangled "spaghetti," 12
   tension, 14, 23, 28
   when to replace, 12
   winding, 19–23

T
Three-Leaf Clover, 30, 43, 59
Thumb Start, 21
Tidal Wave, 57
tournament yo-yo shape, 8
transaxle yo-yo, 9
Two-Finger Start, 22

U
UFO (aka Sleeping Beauty, Flying
   Saucer), 36–37

V
videos, 60

W
Walk the Cat, 56
Walk the Dog, 4, 27
Walk the Duck, 54
Walking the Plank, 23
websites, 39, 57, 60

Y
yo-yos. *See also specific headings*
   care of, 12, 14
   fixing problems with, 13, 14, 23, 28
   hazards, 11, 14, 33, 55
   parts of, 8
   physics of motion, 10
   prices of, 5
   professionals, 6
   questions about, answered, 5–6
   records, 6
   resources for, 60
   speed of, 6
   types of, 8–9

More Good Books
from Williamson Publishing

Please see page 64 for ordering information or to visit our website. Thank you.

American Bookseller Pick of the Lists
Oppenheim Toy Portfolio Best Book Award
Parents' Choice Approved
SUMMER FUN!
60 Activities for a Kid-Perfect Summer
by Susan Williamson

American Bookseller Pick of the Lists
Dr. Toy Best Vacation Product
KIDS' CRAZY ART CONCOCTIONS
50 Mysterious Mixtures for Art & Craft Fun
by Jill Frankel Hauser

Parents' Choice Approved
Parent's Guide Children's Media Award
MAKING COOL CRAFTS &
AWESOME ART!
A Kids' Treasure Trove of Fabulous Fun
by Roberta Gould

Parents' Choice Approved
KIDS' ART WORKS!
Creating with Color, Design, Texture
& More
by Sandi Henry

Parents' Choice Honor Award
THE KIDS' NATURAL HISTORY BOOK
Making Dinos, Fossils, Mammoths & More
by Judy Press

American Bookseller Pick of the Lists
Benjamin Franklin Best
  Education/Teaching Book Award
2000 American Institute of Physics
  Science Writing Award
GIZMOS & GADGETS
Creating Science Contraptions that
Work (& Knowing Why)
by Jill Frankel Hauser

American Bookseller Pick of the Lists
Oppenheim Toy Portfolio Best Book Award
Benjamin Franklin Best Juvenile
  Nonfiction Award
SUPER SCIENCE CONCOCTIONS
50 Mysterious Mixtures for Fabulous Fun
by Jill Frankel Hauser

Parents' Choice Gold Award
American Bookseller Pick of the Lists
Oppenheim Toy Portfolio Best Book Award
THE KIDS' MULTICULTURAL
ART BOOK
Art & Craft Experiences from Around
the World
by Alexandra M. Terzian

The Kids' Guide to
FIRST AID
All about Bruises, Burns, Stings, Sprains
& Other Ouches
by Karen Buhler Gale, R.N.